SEA TURTLES

Life Cycles

ABDO
Publishing Company

A Buddy Book
by **Julie Murray**

VISIT US AT
www.abdopublishing.com

Published by ABDO Publishing Company, 4940 Viking Drive, Edina, Minnesota 55435.

Printed in the United States.

Coordinating Series Editor: Sarah Tieck
Contributing Editor: Michael P. Goecke
Graphic Design: Deb Coldiron
Cover Photograph: Photos.com
Interior Photographs/Illustrations: Animals Animals - Earth Scenes: Klaus Uhlenhut (pages 13, 21); Fotosearch; Minden Pictures: Tui De Roy (page 7), Frans Lanting (page 10), Mitsuaki Wago (page 15, 21), Norbert Wu (page 21); Photodisc; Photos.com

Library of Congress Cataloging-in-Publication Data

Murray, Julie, 1969–
    Sea turtles / Julie Murray.
        p. cm. — (Life Cycles)
    Includes bibliographical references and index.
    ISBN-13: 978-1-59928-711-9
    ISBN-10: 1-59928-711-0
    1. Sea turtles—Life Cycles—Juvenile literature. I. Title.

QL666.C536.M87 2007
597.92'8—dc22
                                                        2006034608

Table Of Contents

What Is A Life Cycle?

Sea turtles are living things. The world is made up of many kinds of life. People are alive. So are cats, dogs, bats, and palm trees.

Sea turtles glide through ocean waters.

Every living thing has a life cycle. A life cycle is made up of many changes and processes. During a life cycle, living things are born, they grow, and they reproduce. And eventually, they die. Different living things start life and grow up in unique ways.

What do you know about the life cycle of sea turtles?

Meet The Sea Turtle

There are seven different species of sea turtles. These include loggerheads, green turtles, leatherbacks, hawksbills, Kemp's ridleys, olive ridleys, and flatbacks.

The sea turtle is a reptile. It has flippers for swimming, a shell for protection, and a beak for eating.

Sea turtles spend a lot of time in water. But, they breathe air.

Each species has unique colors, and markings. And, they are shaped differently. Sea turtles also range in size. The olive ridley weighs about 100 pounds (45 kg). The leatherback can weigh up to 1,300 pounds (590 kg)!

Sea turtles live in warm waters around the world. This includes waters near the United States, Australia, and Mexico.

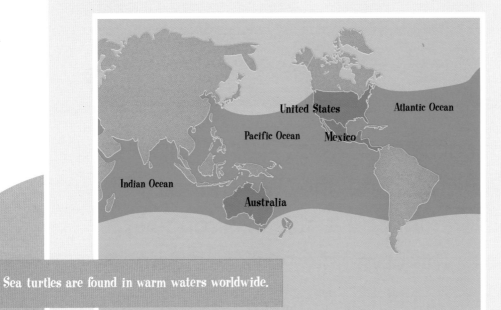

United States

Atlantic Ocean

Pacific Ocean

Mexico

Indian Ocean

Australia

Sea turtles are found in warm waters worldwide.

A Sea Turtle's Life

A sea turtle's life begins in an egg. After a time, the baby sea turtle hatches. Then it digs out of its nest and heads for water.

The young sea turtle lives in the ocean. There, it grows into an adult and migrates. In time, its life ends.

Guess What?

…Six of seven sea turtle species are on the endangered animals list. This list identifies animal species at risk of dying out.

An olive ridley sea turtle lays her eggs.

…When female sea turtles lay eggs, it looks like they are crying. But, this is actually how sea turtles get extra salt out of their body. Sea turtles "cry" whether they are on land or in the ocean.

…Male sea turtles rarely go ashore after leaving the beach at birth!

…Sea turtles can sleep deep underwater! However, some sleep on the water's surface, while others hide under ledges and rocks.

Adult sea turtles can sleep underwater for more than two hours without breathing.

Starting To Grow

To reproduce, a male and female sea turtle mate. Then, the female swims to shore to lay her eggs. She goes to the same beach to nest year after year.

To lay her eggs, a female sea turtle crawls out of the ocean and on to the beach.

The eggs of a flatback sea turtle.

The female buries her eggs in the sand. To do this, she uses her flippers and her body to make a hole. This process is called nesting and is usually done at night.

When the nest is ready, the female lays 50 to 200 soft eggs. Then she goes back to the ocean. The mother sea turtle will never return to the nest.

From Egg To Sea Turtle

The amount of time before sea turtle eggs hatch depends on how warm the sand is. Usually, the eggs hatch after about 60 days.

Baby sea turtles must break out of their shells on their own. To do this, they use a special tooth called a caruncle. The caruncle falls out shortly after birth!

Next, the baby sea turtles dig their way out of the nest. Then, they head for water. There are many dangers for baby sea turtles. So, they must focus on staying safe.

Baby sea turtles, such as this loggerhead, don't get any help from their mothers when they hatch.

Life As An Adult

Scientists have studied sea turtles to see where they swim. Adult sea turtles spend much of their time migrating. Sea turtles are known to use ocean currents to swim in big circles. In this way, they can visit different parts of the oceans.

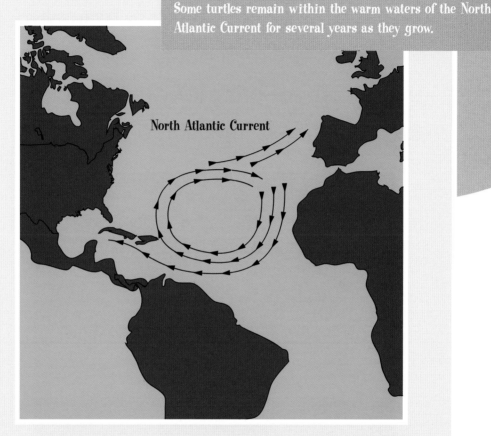

Some turtles remain within the warm waters of the North Atlantic Current for several years as they grow.

North Atlantic Current

Sea turtles have an outstanding ability to navigate water. They know their exact location and how to get to other places.

Adult sea turtles also spend time reproducing and working to stay alive. They have to watch out for certain animals. There are many man-made dangers for sea turtles, too.

Man-made objects, such as fishing nets, can harm sea turtles.

Killer whales sometimes prey on sea turtles.

Endings And Beginnings

Sea turtles have different life spans. Some can live for more than 100 years!

Sea turtles grow the most in their first five to ten years. After that, they grow at a much slower rate.

Death is the end of one sea turtle's life. But, it is not the end of the species. Because sea turtles can reproduce, their species continues on.

Every time a sea turtle hatches from an egg, it helps create a new generation of sea turtles. This is the beginning of another life cycle.

Can You Guess?

Q: What is the upper part of a sea turtle's shell called?
A: The carapace.

Q: How old are the earliest known sea turtle fossils?
A: Scientists have sea turtle fossils that are more than 150 million years old!

Each sea turtle has a unique carapace.

Important Words

generation   a group that is living at the same time and is about the same age.

mate   to engage in an act that leads to reproduction.

migrate   to move from one place to another.

navigate   to find the way from place to place.

process   a way of doing something.

reproduce   to produce offspring, or children.

species   living things that are very much alike.

unique   different.

Web Sites

To learn more about sea turtles, visit ABDO Publishing Company on the World Wide Web. Web site links about sea turtles are featured on our Book Links page. These links are routinely monitored and updated to provide the most current information available.

www.abdopublishing.com

Index